**W9-BDM-009**

*People of the Ancient World*

# THE
# ANCIENT
# GREEKS

WRITTEN BY

ALLISON LASSIEUR

Franklin Watts
A Division of Scholastic Inc.
New York Toronto London Auckland Sydney

**Note to readers:** Definitions for words in **bold** can be found in the Glossary at the back of this book.

Photographs © 2004: AKG-Images, London: 82 (Peter Connolly), 6, 49, 96 bottom left (John Hios), 37, 94 (Pirozzi), 16, 23, 63, 69, 96 bottom center, 100 top; Art Resource, NY: 59 (Bildarchiv Preussischer Kulturbesitz), 65, 70, 71, 80, 90, 95 bottom (Erich Lessing), 85 (Reunion des Musees Nationaux), 99 bottom, 99 center, 99 top (Scala); Bridgeman Art Library International Ltd., London/New York: 22 (Ancient Art and Architecture Collection Ltd.), 42, 43, 97 top, 100 center (Julian Hartnoll/Private Collection), 101 bottom (Museo Archeologico Nazionale, Naples, Italy), 98 top (Museo Capitolino, Rome, Italy), 53 (Staatliche Museen, Berlin, Germany), 67, 96 top left (The Stapleton Collection); Corbis Images: 27 (Archivo Iconografico, S.A.), 60 (Dave Bartruff), 21, 95 top right, 100 bottom, 101 center (Bettmann), 4 center, 91 (Wolfgang Kaehler), 52 (Roger Wood), 9; Hulton|Archive/Getty Images: 26, 31; North Wind Picture Archives: 12, 13, 24, 34, 35, 46, 97 bottom right, 97 bottom left, 98 center, 98 bottom; Robertstock.com/Zefa/Key-Color: 74; Stock Montage, Inc.: 38; Superstock, Inc./Pallas de Velletri: 18; The Image Works: 17 (ARPL/Topham), 44, 58, 95 top left, 96 bottom right, 101 top (The British Museum/Topham-HIP), 29 (Science Museum, London/Topham-HIP); Time Life Pictures/Getty Images/The Mansell Collection: 76, 77, 96 top right; TRIP Photo Library: 72 (Peter Richards), 62 (H. Rogers), 87 (Helene Rogers), 54, 55 (Adina Tovy).

**Cover art by Tatiana Romanova-Grant**
**Map art by XNR Productions Inc.**

Library of Congress Cataloging-in-Publication Data

Lassieur, Allison.
    The ancient Greeks / Allison Lassieur.
        p. cm. — (People of the ancient world)
    Includes bibliographical references and index.
     ISBN 0-531-12339-1 (lib. bdg.)          0-531-16739-9 (pbk.)
    1. Greece—Civilization—To 146 B.C.—Juvenile literature. I. Title. II. Series.
    DF77.L337 2004
    938—dc22

                                                                2004001942

# Contents

# A BARREN, ROCKY OUTCROPPING RISES OUT OF THE MODERN CITY OF ATHENS.

It is called the Acropolis. On it sits the crumbling remains of the Parthenon, one of the world's most recognizable structures. The Parthenon was a temple dedicated to Athena, the patron goddess of the city of Athens. In ancient times, people throughout Greece traveled to the Parthenon to gaze at its brightly painted friezes and its magnificent sculptures. From the Acropolis, visitors could look out over the city of Athens.

Today, the Parthenon is in ruins. Its cracked columns reach into the air, no longer supporting the roof that has long since disappeared. Tourists, not worshippers, now make their way up the steep slopes of the Acropolis. But they still marvel at the Parthenon, just as the ancient Greeks did thousands of years ago.

To many people, the Parthenon represents ancient Greece. When it was built, the Greek civilization was thriving. Back then, Greece was a collection of city-states rather than one unified country. Greek citizens from all areas contributed to the culture of this ancient civilization in many ways. Brilliant scientists and thinkers explored new fields of science, such as astronomy, and made great discoveries in other fields, such as mathematics. In some Greek city-states, leaders created and nurtured a new kind of government called a **democracy**, in which almost every citizen

The Parthenon is located on the Acropolis in Greece. The temple included sculptures that pictured myths and historical events. Today a replica of the Parthenon can be seen in Nashville, Tennessee.

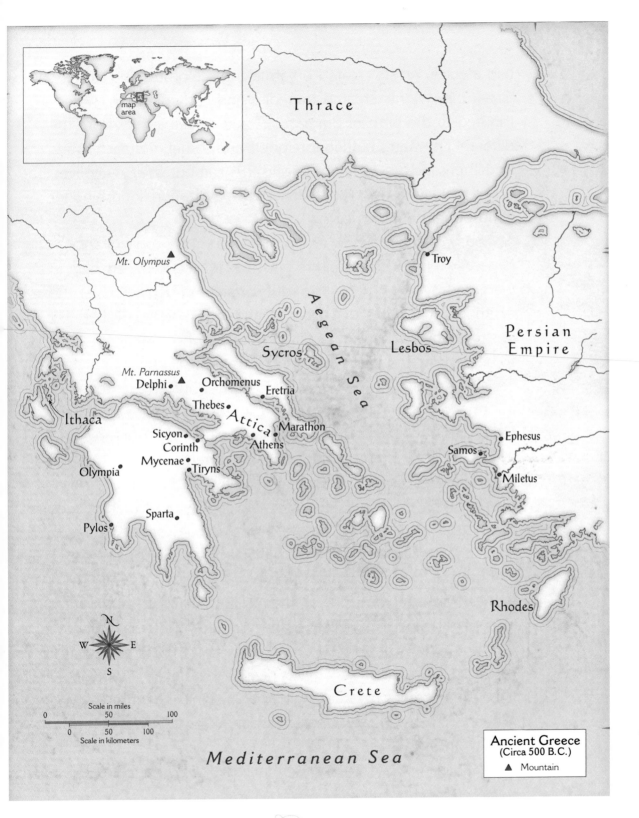

Thrace

Mt. Olympus ▲

• Troy

Aegean Sea

Sycros

Lesbos

Persian
Empire

Mt. Parnassus
Delphi • ▲        • Orchomenus
        • Eretria
Thebes •
            Attica      • Marathon
Sicyon •        Athens •
Corinth •
Mycenae • • Tiryns

Ithaca

Olympia •

Samos •        • Ephesus

• Miletus

Sparta •

Pylos •

Rhodes

N
W    E
S

Scale in miles
0      50      100
0   50   100
Scale in kilometers

Crete

Ancient Greece
(Circa 500 B.C.)
▲ Mountain

Mediterranean Sea

map
area

had a voice. Artists created breathtaking sculptures and pottery. Greek playwrights created tragedies and comedies, which contributed to the birth of dramatic theater. Greek armies from the different city-states battled foreigners and sometimes each other. And thousands of ordinary Greeks went about their daily lives, doing the day-to-day work that kept the civilization flourishing for almost one thousand years.

Today, historians know few details about the people of ancient Greece. Much of their culture and the artifacts they left behind were destroyed long ago through warfare and neglect. Over the centuries, many precious objects and books were deliberately destroyed by invaders and Christian leaders who considered them to be **pagan**, and against the teachings of the Catholic Church.

Modern historians and archaeologists must piece together information from different places to get a full picture of ancient Greek life. Archaeologists have excavated Greek structures and found artifacts. These structures, such as temples and theaters, give clues about the engineering skills of the Greeks. Also, builders for the Roman Empire copied the styles of many Greek buildings in their own architecture, and archaeologists can study the Roman buildings that have survived to gain insight into Greek architecture. Greek pottery, which was often decorated with scenes from everyday life, is an excellent source of information about life in ancient Greece. Marine archaeologists have discovered the wrecks of ancient Greek ships and the remains of the cargo they carried. These objects give further details about Greek life. Roman copies of Greek sculptures that have been destroyed allow historians to study Greek art styles. Many literary works written by ancient Greek scholars that were later copied by others have survived. These works describe and explain many aspects of Greek culture.

Sparta was one of the most powerful city-states. This photograph shows some of the city's ruins.

## The Mysterious Mycenaean Culture

The Mycenaeans inhabited the region that is now called Greece between about 1700–1300 B.C. Theirs is one of the most mysterious ancient cultures because so little of its artifacts have survived for modern historians and archaeologists to study. However, most scholars agree that the Mycenaeans were probably the earliest Greek culture.

Based on archaeological finds and records kept by the ancient Greeks, scientists know that the Mycenaeans built strong, fortified city centers that were surrounded by farmland. These cities, which included Mycenae, Pylos, Tiryns, Thebes, and Orchomenos, were filled with structures that were lavishly decorated with beautiful painted **frescoes**. Archaeologists have found Mycenaean graves filled with gold objects, suggesting that the culture had a wealthy elite class. The most famous archaeological grave finds from this culture were discovered in the nineteenth century by a German archaeologist named Heinrich Schliemann. He unearthed shaft graves dating to the sixteenth century B.C. that were filled with remarkable artifacts and golden objects, including the famous mask of Agamemnon. Other Mycenaean artifacts include jewelry and pottery.

Archaeologists have also found clay tablets inscribed with an early script that historians call Linear B. This script was used to record the language of the Mycenaean culture, although it was used mainly to record accounting information and inventories. No literature or other writings written in Linear B have been discovered, which suggests that the Mycenaeans did not use it for anything other than business.

The Mycenaeans traded with people of other cultures throughout the Mediterranean. Mycenaean artifacts have been found in places as far away as modern Turkey, along the Nile River in Egypt, in Syria, and in Italy. Such far-flung trade routes suggests that the Mycenaeans had a sophisticated culture that could support a complex trading system.

## The Collapse of the Mycenaean Culture and the Dark Age of Greece

In about 1300 B.C., an event created a shift in Mycenaean culture. Historians and archaeologists are unclear about what might have happened. However, at that time, the Mycenaeans stopped building elaborate tombs and palaces and began to build more fortifications for their cities. This suggests that they were preparing for war. Later, many of the Mycenaean cities were burned, such as Orchomenos and Pylos. Between about 1300 and 1100 B.C., almost every Mycenaean city was destroyed. By the end of this time period, the Mycenaean culture had completely collapsed. One of the only sites to escape destruction during this time was the area around what is now Athens.

Scholars do not know what caused the destruction of Mycenaeans. Later, ancient Greek scholars blamed it on invasions by a culture they called the Dorians. However, archaeologists have found very little material evidence to support that idea. They do agree that some kind of warfare or invasion, or perhaps a wave of invasions over a long period of time, wiped out the society.

The time from about 1100–900 B.C. is known as the Dark Age of Greek civilization. Archaeologists have found almost no structures of any kind that date to this time. Objects of beauty, such as jewelry and paintings, are rare. The written script of the Mycenaeans, Linear B, vanished. Scientists continue to debate the reasons why these people could have suffered such a total devastation.

### Archaic Greece

By the eighth century B.C., the civilization had begun to recover. A century before, art began to flourish once again. The Greeks borrowed a new alphabet from another culture, the Phoenicians, and began using it to write in their own language. The Olympic Games were established in 776 B.C. In the hundred years between about 750–650 B.C., writing became widespread throughout the Greek world. The people began to build temples and other structures. Also around this time, in about 750 B.C., Greek civilization

seemed to explode with activity. The population increased dramatically. Archaeologists can determine this by studying numbers of graves dug in a given time period in a given area. Scholars also know about this renewed activity from the writings of later Greeks and from the numerous archaeological finds that date to this time. New structures, such as the temple of Hera and the temple of Aphasia, were constructed. Many historians believe that Homer wrote the **epic poems** *Iliad* and the *Odyssey* during this time.

### The Greek Victory in the Persian War

In the mid-sixth century B.C., most of the Greek city-states on the coast of Asia Minor came under the control of the Persian Empire. In 499 B.C., the city-states rebelled against the Persians and asked other Greek city-states to help them. Only Athens and Eretria agreed. The Greeks were badly outnumbered, and the Persians easily squashed the revolt. But the Persian rulers wanted to get revenge against the city-states that had helped the rebels. Persian armies destroyed Eretria and then sailed to Athens, landing on the plain of Marathon. There, a small Athenian force waited for them.

It should have been an easy victory for the Persians. But instead, the Athenian army defeated the Persians in a great victory. According to some accounts, the

The Battle of Marathon in 490 B.C. was a stunning victory for the Athenians. Legend says that a Greek soldier named Pheidippides ran 22 miles to Athens to report the victory. He is thought to have shouted "Rejoice! We conquer!", then collapsed and died.

Persians lost about 6,400 soldiers, while the Athenians lost only about 192. The Battle of Marathon is considered to be one of the greatest military victories in history. Had the Greeks lost the battle, they would have come under Persian control. For the Athenians, the Battle of Marathon was a great achievement. From that time on, they began to consider themselves to be living in the center of Greek civilization.

After the war, Greeks rebuilt their glorious city-states and ushered in the age of Classical Greece. Although ancient Greece was broken into many city-states, it was in Athens that the culture and society flourished most. This was an age of new confidence in the Greek people. Democracy grew during this time. Great buildings, such as the Parthenon, were constructed. Scientists formed new ideas about astronomy, nature, politics, and philosophy.

The Classical Age lasted for almost two hundred years. At the end of the fourth century B.C., the Greeks were conquered by Alexander the Great, a military leader from Macedonia who eventually conquered much of the world. Greece became just a small part of Alexander's vast world empire.

## Hellenistic Greece

The death of Alexander in 323 B.C. marked the beginning of the Hellenistic Age of ancient Greece. Alexander's generals fought one another to seize as much of his empire as they could. After almost fifty years of fighting, three of the most powerful generals established their kingdoms. Macedonia and Greece were under the control of Antigonus. Egypt became the kingdom of Ptolemy. The old Persian Empire, which included modern-day Turkey, Iran, Syria, Iraq, and central Asia, was ruled by Seleucus.

Greece continued to be an important center for learning and culture, but it never again achieved the greatness it enjoyed during the Classical Age. Some of the greatest discoveries in medicine, astronomy, and literature occurred during the Hellenistic Age. Doctors began to understand the anatomy of the human body through study and dissection. Scholars created standard versions of poetry and literature.

Eventually, however, the Greek culture was overwhelmed by foreign invaders. A new culture, the Roman civilization from central Italy, was rising to power. The Romans would eventually gain control of Greece. By the fourth century A.D., the once-grand Greek civilization had declined.

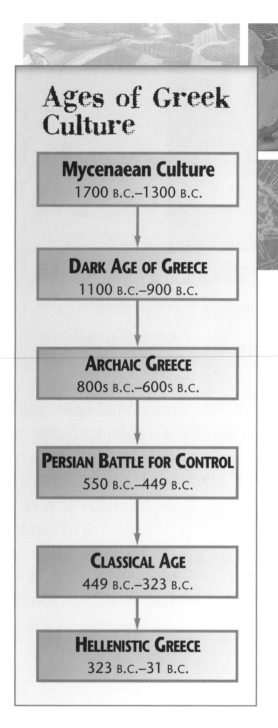

## Ages of Greek Culture

**Mycenaean Culture**
1700 B.C.–1300 B.C.

**DARK AGE OF GREECE**
1100 B.C.–900 B.C.

**ARCHAIC GREECE**
800s B.C.–600s B.C.

**PERSIAN BATTLE FOR CONTROL**
550 B.C.–449 B.C.

**CLASSICAL AGE**
449 B.C.–323 B.C.

**HELLENISTIC GREECE**
323 B.C.–31 B.C.

## Chapter I

# PEOPLE OF THE GOVERNMENT

Ancient Greek civilization held power in the world for more than one thousand years. Ancient Greece was never a unified country with one leader. Instead, Greece was divided into many small units called city-states. Each city-state was known as a **polis**. Each polis controlled its own land, and had its own citizens, and had the freedom to decide what kind of government it would establish. Some of the city-states became democracies. Others followed different governmental systems, such as **oligarchies** or **tyrannies**.

The governments of Greece grew and changed along with the people. Leaders included kings, tyrants, and warriors. Each made his mark on the culture of Greece. Some made changes that would eventually create the world's first and strongest democracy.

## Early Greek Rulers

During the early centuries of Greek civilization, many city-states were ruled by a **basileus**, who was a king, tribal leader, or chieftain. Few details are known about the role of the *basileis*. Historians believe that rule of a particular area

The archaeologist Heinrich Schliemann found this golden mask at Mycenae. It became known as the Mask of Agamemnon. It can be found at the National Archaeology Museum of Athens.

or city-state was passed down through the wealthiest Greek families.

The greatest source of information about the early rulers of the city-states is Greek myths and legends. The *Iliad* and the *Odyssey*, epic poems believed to have been written by the Greek writer Homer sometime in the seventh century B.C., are fiction, but they include many rich details and descriptions of early kings and heroes, which scholars suspect might be based on facts.

Athena was the patron godess of the city of Athens.

Agamemnon, whom Homer calls the king of the Mycenaeans, is one of the most famous Greek monarchs from the poems.

Other writings mention two ancient kings of Athens, Erechtheus and Theseus. In these stories, Erechtheus founded the Great Panathenaea festival, an important celebration dedicated to the birthday of the goddess Athena. Theseus was the son of another Athenian king, Aegeus. His most famous adventure involved slaying the minotaur in the kingdom of Crete. Later, according to the myths, he became king of Athens. The Greek writer Thucydides credited Theseus with uniting many smaller towns, making Athens a powerful city-state. It is unclear whether these two monarchs actually existed, because they appear as characters in Greek legends. However, historians do believe that the Greek writers included real people and events in their works. Scholars can study these fictional writings to get a general idea of what Greek society, culture, and attitudes might have been like.

## Oligarchs and Tyrants

Gradually, the Greek monarchy was replaced by a form of government called an oligarchy. Oligarchy means "ruled by a few." The Greek city-state of Sparta was an exception. It retained its kings for several centuries.

The power of the king was transferred to a small group of men chosen from the wealthiest Greek families. By the end of the eighth century B.C., the oligarchy in Athens was composed of three elected magistrates. The **eponymous archon** was a civil judge and the most powerful of the three leaders. The **king archon** managed the religious affairs of the city-state. The commander in chief of the military forces was the **polemarch**. There was also the **ecclesia**, or the assembly. There is little information on who could join the ecclesia, but scholars suspect that at first, membership was restricted to wealthy landowners and warriors.

From about 670 B.C. to 500 B.C., another kind of government rose alongside the oligarchy: tyranny. A tyrant is a ruler who illegally seizes military power. There is little existing information on individual tyrants, although scholars have pieced together some clues from ancient Greek writings. Some tyrants, such as Cypselus of Corinth, who ruled from 657–627 B.C., and Orthagoras of Sicyon, who ruled in the mid-seventh century B.C., were former polemarches. Cylon of Athens, who tried to take over Athens in 632 B.C. and failed, was a famous Olympic champion. One of the most famous Greek tyrants was Polycrates of Samos. In about 535 B.C., he took over the government of Samos while its citizens were outside the city walls celebrating the festival of Hera.

Tyrannies were not always bad. Most tyrants wanted to be good leaders in their city-states, so they encouraged trade and supported many construction projects. Many Greeks also saw the rule of tyrants as a relief from the rule of the wealthy nobles. The Greek philosopher Aristotle mentioned this in his work *Politics*, saying, "A tyrant is set up . . . to oppose the notables so that the people may suffer no injustice from them."

Most tyrannies were short-lived, lasting for only a generation or two. Then another military leader or a wealthy Greek aristocrat would overthrow the tyranny and start his own. But regardless who was the tyrant, all of the power in society remained in the hands of the rich elite. Poorer Greeks had no power. Farmers went into debt and lost their land. Thousands of Greeks were forced to sell themselves into slavery to survive. The economy began to suffer. By the early sixth century B.C., Athens was on the brink of revolution and civil war.

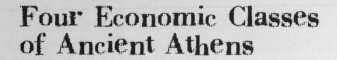

## Four Economic Classes of Ancient Athens

| | |
|---|---|
| *Pentakosiomedimnoi* | Wealthy aristocrats |
| *Hippada telountes* | Knights |
| *Zeugiatai* | Farmers |
| *Thetes* | Poorest Athenians |

### Solon, Cleisthenes, and the Development of Democracy

In an effort to avoid violence, the Athenians elected a former magistrate, Solon, as mediator in 594 B.C. Today scholars credit Solon with transforming Athenian society and paving the way for democracy.

One of Solon's first acts as leader was to abolish the debts of thousands of Athenian citizens. He repealed the laws that allowed people to sell themselves into slavery to repay debts. Solon then created four economic classes.

Solon opened up many government offices to people from the different classes for the first time. The thetes could meet to discuss and vote on various matters. For the first time, heritage was no longer a qualification for holding an office. All Athenian men could have a say in government. Women were not allowed to participate in government, nor were other members of society, such as slaves and **metics** (foreign-born residents of Athens).

A second leader, Cleisthenes, continued to create laws that strengthened democracy. From 508 to 502 B.C., he enacted a series of reforms meant to break the power of the rich families

once and for all. He decreed that all citizens of Athens could be part of the assembly. He created ten new groups, or tribes, of Athenians by dividing the city-state geographically. He then established a council of five hundred men, called the **boule**, which included fifty members from each of the ten tribes. Every free male citizen over the age of thirty could be part of the council, and members were chosen by lot.

This nineteenth century woodcut shows the early Greek leader Solon speaking about his laws. Solon was known as the Lawgiver to early Athenians. The Greek writer Plutarch wrote that Solon once said, "Justice, even if slow, is sure."

# The Pnyx

The assembly met in the open on a hill known as the Pnyx. The Pnyx includes an outdoor auditorium, stairways, and walls. Two walkways called **stoas** sheltered people during bad weather. The Pnyx also included a sanctuary to the god Zeus.

Zeus was the supreme god in Greek mythology and a powerful deity to the Greek people. In 1910, archaeologists found and excavated the Pnyx. Today the remains of the Pnyx can be seen about a mile west of the Acropolis.

Today, the Pnyx is a small hill surrounded by parkland. This large, flat stone platform is set in its side. In ancient Greece the assembly met on the Pnyx. The platform was the bema, or speaker's platform. The grassy area in front of the bema was once bare rock where as many as six thousand men could stand and listen.

By the end of the sixth century B.C., Athens had a strong new governmental system. The people began to prosper, and the city-state grew.

## Sparta, the Military City-State

The vast majority of information about ancient Greece is focused on the city-state of Athens. Most of the writings and artwork that have survived came from Athens. Ancient documents describe Athenian politics, people, events, festivals, and other aspects of daily life. Athenian writers seldom bothered to describe events or people from other city-states, unless they somehow had an impact on Athenian life. For this reason,

## Pericles, a Great Athenian Leader

Pericles was born into a wealthy family in about 495 B.C. He was a military leader and statesman who became very popular in Athens. Pericles supported a number of political reforms that strengthened Athenian democracy. He established government salaries for public officials and opened more offices to citizens of all classes. Pericles negotiated a truce between Athens and its chief rival, Sparta. Pericles used this time of peace to build Athens into a magnificent city. He encouraged drama, art, and architecture. Under his direction, great temple monuments, such as the Parthenon and the Propylaea on the Acropolis, were constructed. By the time of Pericles' death in 429 B.C., Athens was firmly established as a one of the most powerful Greek city-states.

This hand-colored woodcut shows the marketplace in Sparta, a powerful Greek city-state. Spartan culture focused mainly on the military and warfare. Soldiers were taught to shun luxuries. Today, the word *spartan* means "basic or bare."

very little information exists about the hundreds of other city-states that thrived in the civilization.

One city-state that did command a lot of attention from the Athenians, however, was Sparta. Sparta and Athens were bitter rivals for much of their history, both militarily and economically. Sparta was primarily a military-focused state for much of its history, and the Spartan army was famous for its skill and sense of duty.

Sparta had a government system both similar to and different from that of Athens. The Spartan constitution provided for a dual

## Ancient Ostra

In 487 B.C., Athenians made an important addition to their democracy. The assembly could vote to expel citizens from the city-state for ten years. To **ostracize** someone, a majority of citizens would vote against a person who was felt to impede the normal work of the government. Sometimes the citizens voted to ostracize power-hungry politicians whom they felt could be a danger to the government. Each citizen scratched the name of the person he wanted ostracized on a piece, or shard, of pottery called an ***ostra***. Thousands of these shards have been discovered, many with names scratched on them.

kingship to lead the city. These two kings had equal power and led military campaigns. But the Spartan government also had elements of a democracy. For example, the **apella** was the Spartan assembly. Men over age eighteen could become part of the apella. The **gerousia** was a group of twenty-eight Spartans, over the age of sixty, which was too old for military service. They controlled most of the public business of Sparta and could veto actions taken by the apella. A council of five magistrates, called **ephors**, watched the kings closely to make sure they did not abuse their power. Ephors had financial, judicial, and administrative powers over the assembly and the gerousia.

The Spartan government was admired by other Greeks for the way it balanced three different systems: monarchy, aristocracy, and democracy.

## Chapter II

# SCIENTISTS
## OF GREECE

It can be argued that the people of ancient Greece invented the idea of scientific study. Many Greek scholars closely observed the natural world and recorded what they saw. From their observations and conclusions sprang such advances in sciences as mathematics, astronomy, and medicine.

### The Greeks and Mathematics

It is difficult to imagine that mathematics was something that needed to be invented. But it was the Greeks who first began to explore what is known as "pure" mathematics. Pure mathematics is the study of the principles of mathematics for their own sake, rather than for their usefulness. The Greeks created many theories, or ideas, of mathematics in areas such as geometry and algebra.

Of all the early Greek mathematicians, the most famous is Euclid of Alexandria. Born in about 325 B.C., Euclid wrote a book called *Elements.* It is considered to be an important work because it established basic ideas about math that no one had ever considered before. For example, Euclid wrote that the shortest distance between two points is a straight line. No one

Euclid said that the shortest distance between two points is a straight line.

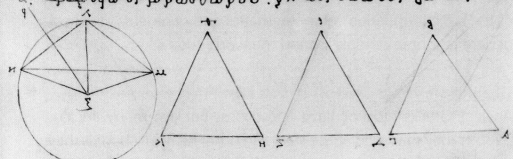

The Greek scientist Euclid is best known for his book on mathematics, the *Elements*. Euclid taught at Alexandria in Egypt sometime in the early third century B.C. This page is from a copy of *Elements*. It shows some of the geometric diagrams that Euclid used in his equations.

had realized this simple fact until Euclid pointed it out. His most famous idea is that if a line is drawn from one point to another, there can only be one other line drawn exactly parallel to that line. These two lines will never meet, no matter how far they extended in either direction. Today these ideas seem very basic. But to the ancient Greeks, they were new and exciting.

Pythagoras of Samos is considered by many to be the world's first pure mathematician. He developed one of the best-known mathematical theorems: the Pythagorean theorem. It states that for a triangle with a right angle, the square of the length of the hypotenuse is equal to the sum of the square of the lengths of the other two sides. This is often written as $a^2+b^2=c^2$. This theorem was probably understood by earlier cultures, such as the Babylonians, but Pythagoras was the first to prove it. Therefore, he is given the credit for it. The theorem is important because it is one of the basic foundations of mathematics and geometry. His theories are taught in schools around the world today.

## Greek Scientists Decipher the Sky

Ancient Greeks did not have telescopes. But like many ancient people, they marveled at the stars and other heavenly bodies they could see with the naked eye, including the Sun, the moon, Mercury, Venus, Mars, Jupiter, and Saturn. They noticed that the brightest lights in the sky moved. They called these moving lights *planetos*, which means "wanderer" in Greek.

One of the most famous Greek astronomers was Pythagoras, the creator of the Pythagorean theorem. Although he believed that Earth was a sphere in the center of a group of hollow

Euclid is best known for explaining that two parallel lines will never meet regardless of their length.

spheres, which it is not, he did correctly theorize that Earth was round. He was also the first to realize that the planet Venus that could be seen in the morning sky was the same as the planet Venus that could be seen in the night sky.

Other Greeks made astounding advances in the understanding of the sky. Anaxagoras, born about in 500 B.C., was the first to realize that the moon's light was "false," meaning that it reflected the light of the sun rather than giving off a light of its own. Heracleides of Ponticus, who lived during the late fourth century B.C., suggested that Earth rotates on its axis daily. Aristarchus of Samos, who was born about 310 B.C., was the first to maintain that Earth rotates and revolves around the Sun, and the first to attempt to measure the distances between the Sun, Earth, and the moon.

Pythagoras was a famous Greek philosopher and mathematician. He is best known for a mathematical equation now known as the Pythagoran theorm. Pythagoras founded a philosophical and religious school in the Greek city of Croton.

## The Doctors of Greece

Ideas about healing the body were in existence before the Greek civilization flourished. Other ancient civilizations, such as the Egyptian civilization, had individuals who practiced medicine. However, many of their ideas about medicine included magic and superstition, with only some knowledge about how the

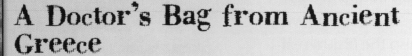

## A Doctor's Bag from Ancient Greece

Greek doctors carried most of their medical instruments with them in small wooden chests. Many of these boxes have survived. Archaeologists have found a variety of medical tools inside these chests, such as scalpels and probes. These items were stored in small compartments inside the chest.

human body actually functioned. Greek scholars were the first to begin compiling information about healing and medicine. They observed the symptoms of many diseases and struggled to understand and treat sickness.

Asclepius may have been one of the earliest Greek physicians. Scholars think he might have been a real person, but there is no evidence to prove this. Little is known about his life, although scholars think he lived in about 1200 B.C. Many temples and shrines were dedicated to Asclepius, and he eventually became known as the god of medicine. His temples, called **asclepions**, became very important to the Greeks. Patients would bring offerings to the temple and be treated by the priests, who were healers. In some cases, medical schools connected to these temples trained new healers. Asclepius's symbol was a serpent wrapped around a staff. A similar image is still used today as a symbol for healing.

Hippocrates gained fame in the late fifth century B.C. as the greatest physician of his time. He accurately described symptoms of diseases such as epilepsy and pneumonia. He advocated diet, exercise, rest, and cleanliness as important to good health. The beliefs of Hippocrates are the basis of an oath for physicians to follow that is still used today.

Hippocrates founded a medical school on the island of Cos. His writings were part of the school's general texts. Hippocrates revolutionized the way people viewed medicine and sickness because he believed that medicine was not a philosophy, or a way

This ancient Greek sculpture, called a bas-relief, shows a physician examining a patient. The figure on the right is Hippocrates, the father of medicine. He is holding a snake coiled around a staff in his left hand. This became the symbol of medicine.

of thinking. He advocated clinical observations, diagnosis, and prognosis. Hippocrates believed that diseases had specific causes. He was among the first physicians to rely on physical examinations of patients to determine and try to treat ailments. Today Hippocrates is known as the father of medicine.

Some of the theories proposed by Greek scientists were later proved to be wrong. Also, much of their work was dismissed and ignored by later cultures that preferred to rely on religious ideas rather than on scientific observation and study. But even though many of their theories were incorrect, the fact that they proposed them showed that the Greeks were trying to understand, through scientific study, how the world around them worked.

# GREEK ATHLETES AND SPORTS

Few people in history have attached more importance to physical conditioning than the ancient Greeks did. The Greeks delighted in the strength and health of the human body. Hundreds of surviving Greek sculptures depict the beautifully formed bodies of both men and women. Greek paintings show naked athletes, their muscles rippling as they run, jump, fight, and wrestle.

## Athletic Training Centers

Archaeologists have unearthed ancient sports training areas throughout Greece. Most of them include a **palaestra**, or wrestling school, a gymnasium, and sometimes a stadium in which athletic competitions were held. The number and size of these centers suggest that they were a vital part of life for many Greeks.

Archaeologists have discovered many things about Greek athletics by studying palaestrae ruins. Most palaestrae included a main structure with a changing room, a bathroom, and an equipment storage area. Some also had a large, walled training area, although few of these have survived.

Attending palaestra was an important part of the education of wealthy Greek boys. The boys were entrusted to professional trainers, called **paidotribes**. Paidotribes were responsible for teaching the boys wrestling, boxing, jumping, running, and throwing the javelin and the discus. Sometimes, paidotribes tapped their students with long sticks when their bodies were in the wrong positions for the different sports.

Older boys and men exercised in the gymnasium. Most gymnasiums had exercise rooms, baths, and shrines dedicated to different gods. Although only the foundations

Many Greek cities had a dromos, which was a long open passage enclosed by stone walls. In Sparta, it was the custom for young men to exercise and run in the dromos.

and ruins of the gymnasiums have survived, archaeologists believe that some of the larger ones also had shaded walkways, libraries, gardens, and parks. The gymnasium usually had a large open area in which athletes could practice javelin throwing, discus throwing, and running. Some gymnasiums were built near rivers so the athletes could enjoy a cool bath after their workouts. The word "gymnasium" is from the Greek word *gymnos*, which translates to "naked" or "lightly clad." Historians believe that it was common for Greeks to exercise and play sports in the nude.

Gymnasiums became so popular that traveling teachers known as **sophists** began lecturing there. By the fourth century B.C. gymnasiums had developed into respected schools of learning. Three of the most famous gymnasiums in Greece, the Academy, the Lyceum, and the Cynosarges, were located in Athens. All three began as gymnasiums but eventually became schools in which great philosophers and other learned men lectured.

## The Olympic Games

Historians believe that there were probably hundreds of local athletic festivals held throughout ancient Greece. Most of them were

## Rules of the Olympic Games

Each athletic event in the ancient Olympic Games had its own rules. Some seem harsh by today's standards. In the **pankration**, punching, kicking, choking, and finger breaking were allowed. Biting and eye-gouging were prohibited. Special judges saw to it that rule-breakers were punished. If a runner made a false start in a foot race, he could be whipped.

associated with a religious festival or the worship of a specific god or goddess. Four large festivals were famous throughout ancient Greece. They were the Olympic and Nemean Games, which were held in honor of the god Zeus. The Isthmian Games were held in honor of Poseidon, god of the sea. The Pythian Games were held in honor of Apollo, the god of music and healing.

Of all the major games, the Olympic Games were the most prestigious and the most popular. They were held every four years, from about 776 B.C. to A.D. 393. During the Olympic Games, the entire Greek world agreed to a three-month truce called the **ekecheiria** so that anyone who wanted to travel to the games could do so safely. The games were open to all Greek citizens, which meant all men who were not slaves. Non-Greeks could not compete. Women could not even watch the games, although some virgin priestesses were allowed inside the stadium.

The Olympic Games lasted for five days, some of which were devoted to religious events and sacrifices. According to ancient writers, the Olympic Games included chariot racing, discus

**This powerful, full-sized statue is called "The Discus Thrower." The original was sculpted by a well-known Greek artist named Myron in about 450 B.C.**

A crowd cheers the winner of a chariot race.

throwing, long jumping, javelin throwing, foot races, wrestling competitions, and other events. The Greeks also had pankration contests, which was a sport that combined boxing and wrestling. On the last day of the games, the winners were awarded prizes of olive wreaths.

## Some Famous Ancient Olympic Champions

Winning an event in the ancient Olympic Games made many athletes famous, just as winning one in the modern Olympic Games does today. Winners were allowed to erect statues of themselves in Olympia. Some returned home to parades and feasts in their honor. Today, historians know the names of hundreds of ancient Olympic Games winners and their amazing athletic feats from the engraved bases of statues and from records of the various Olympic Games that have survived.

One of the first athletes to be described in ancient writings was Milo of Croton. In five back-to-back Olympic Games, from 536 B.C. to 520 B.C., he won men's wrestling events. His strength was legendary even in his own time. Milo was said to have carried a four-year-old bull around the Olympic stadium and then eaten it in one day. He was reported to eat twenty pounds of meat, twenty pounds of bread, and eigh-

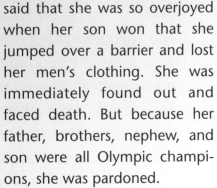

## A Woman at the Olympic Games

Women were forbidden to watch the Olympic Games. The penalty for it was death. According to some ancient accounts, one woman defied the law. Her name was Kallipateira. She disguised herself as a trainer so she could watch her son compete in the games. It is said that she was so overjoyed when her son won that she jumped over a barrier and lost her men's clothing. She was immediately found out and faced death. But because her father, brothers, nephew, and son were all Olympic champions, she was pardoned.

teen pints of wine per day. When he erected his statue in Olympus, he supposedly carried the giant stone statue to its place himself. As a trick, he used to tie a cord around his forehead and then break it by swelling his veins and muscles. When Milo wasn't winning Olympic events, he was a commander in the army.

Legend says that Milo died while testing his own strength. He came across an old cracked tree trunk while walking in the forest. He stepped into the crack and tried to split the wood by pushing it apart with his hands and feet. Instead, the tree snapped closed onto his hands, trapping him. Later, he was eaten by wolves.

Another famous champion was Theagenes of Thasos. According to an inscription at the sacred city of Delphi, Theagenes won boxing and pankration events at the Olympic Games and won boxing events three times at the Pythian Games. He also won boxing events nine times and the pankration once at the Isthmian Games and won boxing events nine times at the Nemean Games. He won the long-distance race at a festival at Argos. The inscription goes on to say that he won 1,300 victories at other events and was unbeaten at boxing for twenty-two years. Little else is known about Theagenes. However, three statues of him were erected throughout Greece: in Delphi, Olympia, and in his hometown of Thasos, suggesting that he had won great fame and glory as a star athlete.

Almost nothing is known about the hundreds of other Greeks who were sports champions. Most of the statues of these athletes were destroyed long ago. All that remains are thousands of statue bases, which are inscribed with the names of many winners and the events they won. The sheer number of these inscribed bases hints at the importance of Greek athletics.

Chapter IV

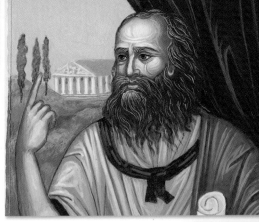

# PHILOSOPHERS AND THINKERS

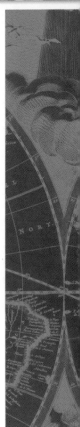

The word "philosophy" combines two Greek words, *philia* ("to love") and *sophia* ("wisdom"). The ancient Greeks explored deep ideas, such as humankind's reason for being on Earth. Greek thinkers examined the way humans interacted with one another and how these relationships affected other things. The Greeks created the discipline of philosophy to explore these ideas. Even today, the ideas first put forward by Greek philosophers continue to be debated.

In some cases, the writings of a Greek philosopher, such as Aristotle, has survived to this day. In other cases, none of the philosopher's work was written down. This was the case with Socrates. The writings of the vast majority of Greek philosophers were destroyed or broken into fragments. Fortunately, many texts were copied and recopied through the centuries, allowing some Greek philosophy to be passed down. Sometimes, one ancient philosopher would copy parts of another philosopher's work into his own for commentary or study

thereby preserving it. Historians piece together these parts to build complete copies of ancient texts when the originals have long since disappeared.

## The Age of Greek Philosophers

Historians generally agree that Greek philosophers remained active for almost a thousand years, from the moment Thales of Miletus predicted a solar eclipse in 529 B.C. to the moment the Christian emperor Justinian outlawed the teaching of pagan, or non-Christian, ideas in A.D. 529. Philosophy was revolutionary

The Italian Renaissance painting *The School of Athens* shows many famous ancient Greek thinkers. Plato is in the center, pointing upward. Beside him is Aristotle. The painting, now in the Vatican in Rome, was restored in the 1990s.

because it enabled some people to explore the world through their intellect and rational thought. Many members of other cultures had struggled to understand their world, but they had done so by inventing religions and myths to explain natural events and human actions. Although the ancient Greeks had a strong belief in their deities, they did not believe that the gods controlled all things. Instead, the Greeks believed that they were free to observe the world and to come up with their own ideas about why things happened as they did.

The people of Athens were in a unique position to embrace

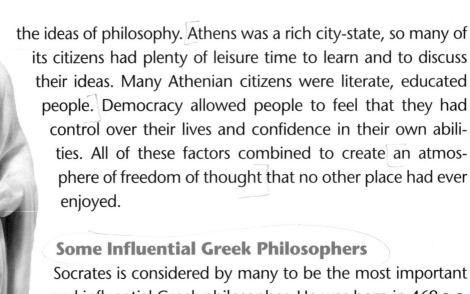

the ideas of philosophy. Athens was a rich city-state, so many of its citizens had plenty of leisure time to learn and to discuss their ideas. Many Athenian citizens were literate, educated people. Democracy allowed people to feel that they had control over their lives and confidence in their own abilities. All of these factors combined to create an atmosphere of freedom of thought that no other place had ever enjoyed.

## Some Influential Greek Philosophers

Socrates is considered by many to be the most important and influential Greek philosopher. He was born in 469 B.C. As a middle-aged man, he decided to become a teacher and to devote the rest of his life to philosophical debate. Socrates believed that the way to gain true knowledge was first to realize that no person could understand the world perfectly. The way to gain knowledge, he thought, was to ask questions that would unlock the secrets of understanding human life. He loved to ask difficult, abstract questions of his followers and others about religion and virtue.

Although his followers adored him, the government thought his ideas were dangerous. In 399 B.C., Socrates was arrested and convicted of treason and corrupting the young, and then sentenced to death. He drank poisonous hemlock and died surrounded by his friends and followers.

Socrates did not write down his thoughts. We know about his work through the writings of his most famous follower, Plato. Plato was a wealthy, educated man. After spending time in the army, Plato became a student of Socrates. After Socrates' death, Plato traveled to Egypt and Italy and studied with other brilliant philosophers from the Pythagorean School, such as Archytas and

**This statue of Socrates shows a short, unattractive man. Socrates' pupils wrote that he was overweight and had big lips and a pug nose. But they admired him for his inner spirit and intelligence. Socrates is considered to be the founder of western philosophy.**

Tarentum. When Plato returned to Athens, he founded a school of learning that became known as the Academy. Many scholars consider it to be Europe's first university-like school. Plato wrote his ideas in the form of conversations called dialogues rather than in straightforward text. In these conversations, characters debate many subjects, such as religion, mathematics, and the natural world.

In 367 B.C., a seventeen-year-old student arrived at Plato's Academy. His name was Aristotle, and he would later become a great philosopher. Little is known about this period in Aristotle's life, other than the fact that he became a teacher at the Academy and stayed there for twenty years. He then left the Academy and traveled extensively. He eventually returned to Athens and founded another school, the Lyceum. According to some ancient accounts, Aristotle lectured on almost every subject taught at the

## Plato's Academy

The Academy was located outside Athens. The ruins of the famous school can be seen today. Modern archaeologists began to excavate the site of the Academy in 1929. Since then, a number of excavations have unearthed most of the school's buildings.

For example, archaeologists discovered that the Academy's gymnasium is a large, rectangular building with rooms on one side. A small room inside was probably used as a palaestra. Another well-known section of the Academy is called the Sacred House. The Sacred House consists of seven rooms on each side of a long hallway. Archaeologists have discovered the remains of sacrifices in the building, which suggests that the rooms were used for religious purposes.

Alexander the Great is among the world's most famous military leaders. When he was a boy, he was tutored by Aristotle. Aristotle taught Alexander to have a love for literature and learning.

Lyceum, including logic, physics, astronomy, zoology, theology, politics, economics, and poetry.

As a philosopher, Aristotle believed that every subject had to be approached with logic. He was the first to create a systematic argument called a syllogism, which consists of two premises and a conclusion and is used to prove a point. Aristotle proposed this idea: Every Greek is a person. Every person is mortal. Therefore, every Greek is mortal. Although this idea seems obvious today, to the Greeks it was an interesting, new concept.

Socrates, Plato, and Aristotle, along with other Athenian and Greek philosophers, changed the way human beings thought about themselves and their world. To the Greeks, philosophy was not about facts or correct answers. It was about discussion and ideas. The Greek philosophers explored all facets of human experience, asking questions and confronting the views of others. Aristotle, for example, believed that all things have a purpose and a function they must perform in order to fulfill it, an idea that many people believe today. Their writings discuss the questions, struggles, and passions that have driven people for thousands of years.

## Chapter V

# PRIESTS, PRIESTESSES, AND GREEK RELIGION

The ancient Greek people were polytheistic, which means they believed in many gods. Ancient Greek civilization worshipped a lively group of gods and goddesses, including the great Zeus; his ever-jealous wife Hera; Apollo, the god of music and healing; mighty Athena, goddess of war and wisdom; Ares, god of war; beautiful Aphrodite, goddess of love; and many others. The Greeks believed the gods were human-like beings who influenced the lives of all Greeks.

Although the Greeks had a group of recognized deities, they did not have an organized religion or religious beliefs. They did not even have a word for "religion" in their language. To the Greek people, the gods were everywhere,

all the time. The Greeks believed that every human action or thought could be influenced by the gods.

The Greeks thought they could show their reverence for the gods through their own actions. The most important thing to a Greek was having the goodwill of the gods. Greeks asked for this by giving objects to the gods in the form of sacrifices. Food, drink,

This frieze from the Parthenon shows Poseidon, Apollo, and Artemis. Poseidon was the god of the sea and one of the most powerful Greek gods. Apollo, the god of music, and Artemis, goddess of the hunt, were brother and sister.

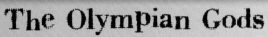

# The Olympian Gods

The Olympians were twelve gods who ruled after the overthrow of the Titans, the children of Uranus, god of the sky, and Gaea, goddess of Earth.

| | |
|---|---|
| **Zeus** | King of the gods; husband and brother of Hera; father of Apollo, Artemis, Athena, Ares, Hermes; brother of Demeter, Hestia, and Poseidon |
| **Hera** | Queen of the gods; wife and sister of Zeus, mother of Ares and Hephaestus; sister to Hestia and Demeter |
| **Athena** | Goddess of war and wisdom; daughter of Zeus |
| **Ares** | God of war; son of Zeus and Hera |
| **Hermes** | Messenger of the gods; son of Zeus |
| **Poseidon** | God of the seas; brother of Zeus |
| **Hephaestus** | Craftsman of the gods; son of Hera and Zeus |
| **Aphrodite** | Goddess of love; daughter of Zeus |
| **Apollo** | God of music and healing; son of Zeus |
| **Artemis** | Goddess of the hunt; daughter of Zeus |
| **Demeter** | Goddess of agriculture; sister of Zeus, Hera, and Hestia |
| **Hestia** | Goddess of the hearth and home; sister of Zeus, Hera, and Demeter |

the blood of animals, and other objects could be sacrificed to the gods. The larger the offering, the more attention the gods paid to the people making the offerings. In most cases, the priests oversaw the offerings in the temples.

## Priests, Priestesses, and Their Duties

There was no official organization of priests and priestesses in ancient Greece. Instead, the priests served as caretakers of the many sacred objects within the temples. They also supervised the official sacrifices and other rituals associated with the specific god of their temple. In Athens, the office of priest was usually a part-time position that was open to anyone, although prostitutes, people in debt, and military officers who had deserted the army were forbidden to hold the position. The temples to the various goddesses were supervised by priestesses, who had much the same qualifications as the priests. Little is known about the priests who worked in other Greek city-states. Historians suspect that the duties of other priests were similar to those of the priests of Athens.

Each town or city-state in Greece had at least one temple dedicated to a specific god or goddess. The Greeks considered these temples to be the homes of the gods rather than places of worship. People brought offerings for the gods or goddesses to their temples. Temples usually held a statue of the gods or goddesses and other objects said to be the possessions of that deity. One of the most famous Greek temples is the Parthenon in Athens. It was built in honor of Athena, the patron goddess of Athens.

Priests were also responsible for organizing and conducting the many festivals dedicated to the gods, although nothing is

The Greeks placed their dead in large stone coffins called sarcophagi. Each sarcophagus was painted with designs and scenes. This scene shows a woman and a pipe-player approaching a table. Another woman, possibly a priestess, makes an offering.

known of their exact duties. These festivals included plays, music, dancing, and sporting contests, along with parades to the temple, large sacrifices to the gods, and lavish feasts.

Little other information about the duties and lives of Greek priests and priestesses exists. Most of what scholars know about them comes from the writings of other ancient Greeks, and most of them did not record many facts about the priests. For example, in Plato's work *The Statesman*, one character says, "There is also the priestly class, who, as the law declares, know how to give the gods gifts from men in the form of sacrifices which are acceptable to them, and to ask on our behalf blessings in return from them."

## The Mysterious Prophecies of the Oracles

Greek priests and priestesses had an important role in another aspect of Greek religion, the oracles. The shrine, the priestess or priest, and the prophecy she or he gave were all considered to be the oracle.

The Greek people visited oracles to ask the gods questions. Special priests and priestesses inside the oracles gave answers by interpreting various signs. For example, at the oracle of Zeus at Dodona, a worshipper first wrote a question on a slab of lead. Then the priest of the oracle listened to the rustling leaves of sacred oak trees to learn the answer. Sometimes, the priests or priestesses gave cryptic answers that were up to the worshipper to figure out.

By far the most famous and respected oracle in Greece was the oracle at Delphi. Historians know its importance from ancient Greek writers, who described it and told stories about how its predictions affected battles and other events. The Greeks considered the location of the oracle to be the center of the world. It was so famous that kings and leaders from other countries sought guidance from the oracle. The oracle at Delphi became a center for political information and news.

The Greek writer Plutarch served as high priest of a temple of Apollo in the first century A.D. He recorded how the oracle worked. A special priestess, known as a **pythia**, sat somewhere

The pythia was the oracle priestess. She gave puzzling, cryptic prophecies that each person had to decipher for themselves. If someone did not like the pythia's prophecies, they might pay the priestess more gold. Then she might give them a different prophecy.

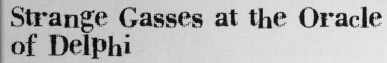

# Strange Gasses at the Oracle of Delphi

Ancient writers recorded that the pythia breathed sweet-smelling fumes that put her into a trance. Until recently, historians dismissed ancient reports of mysterious mists in the oracle at Delphi as fanciful stories. But recent geological surveys suggest that the famous pythian priestesses might have been breathing the fumes of natural gasses when they made their cryptic predictions.

Geologists have discovered that the temple lies on top of a previously undiscovered fault, or crack in Earth's crust. They suspect that earthquake activity might have heated up underground water and created gasses that seeped up into the temple. Scientists speculate that one of the gasses might have been ethylene, which is sweet smelling. Small doses of the gas produce a floating sensation and a sense of happiness, exactly what a priestess might have needed to have visions.

**The oracle at Delphi was the most important and influential shrine in the Greek world. It was built over a sacred stream. People traveled from all over ancient Greece to consult the oracle.**

inside the oracle. (Plutarch did not specify where.) Alongside her were sacred objects that may have included a tomb and a golden statue of the god Apollo. She listened to the questions brought before her and gave answers. Other Greek writers described the pythia going into a trance and relaying messages from Apollo. Many ancient Greeks described strange gasses or

vapors that swirled around the pythia, adding to her mysterious power. It is unclear how the pythia was chosen, or how she got her power.

Today, the religion of the ancient Greeks is little more than fanciful stories. But to the ancient Greeks and to the priests and priestesses who tended the gods, their religion was a real, and vital, aspect of civilization.

# POETS AND PLAYWRIGHTS

The people of ancient Greece created some of the world's most enduring poetry and literature. Philosophers and thinkers expressed their ideas about the world in their writings. Poets wrote ceremonial songs honoring the gods and personal poems about love and passion. As the culture grew and changed, the way Greek people expressed their ideas, thoughts, and dreams changed as well.

## Epic Poetry of the Early Greeks

In early Greece, storytellers traveled from town to town, regaling the townspeople with fabulous tales of brave heroes, bloody battles, and noble kings. They also sometimes wove myths about the gods in with true facts about real events while telling these stories. These long stories became known as epic poems.

Early Greece gave rise to two monumental works of epic poetry, the *Iliad* and the *Odyssey*. Both were written by a famous storyteller named Homer. Little is known about Homer's life. Tradition says that Homer was a wandering, blind poet who told stories about Greece's glorious past.

Today many scholars suspect that the poems were probably written down long after Homer's death, although no one knows for certain who wrote them or when they were first written down.

Both poems recount the events that took place during and after the Trojan War, a war between the ancient Mycenaeans and the people of a town called Troy. The Trojan War was probably fought some time between 1230 B.C. and 1180 B.C. The *Iliad* focuses on the last year of the war and on the formidable warrior Achilles. The *Odyssey* is the story of the warrior Odysseus, who spends ten years trying to get home to his wife after fighting in the Trojan War. Although both stories describe many supernatural elements, such as battles with gods and encounters with mystical and dangerous creatures, most Greeks of the Classical Age considered them to be reasonably accurate accounts of their own ancient history.

Homer's two works, the *Iliad* and the *Odyssey*, are epic poems about the Battle of Troy and the Greek heroes Achilles and Odysseus. No one is sure what Homer looked like. This Roman "portrait" bust is one artist's guess. The statue was designed to be mounted on a square stone shaft.

## The Beautiful Music of the Lyric Poets

The ancient Greeks created another form of poetry known today as lyric poetry. Lyric poetry got its name because it was sung rather than spoken and was usually accompanied by a stringed instrument called a lyre. Scholars believe that lyric poetry has its roots in early Greek culture, when people would create songs for special occasions, such as harvests, weddings, funerals, and other important events.

Unlike epic poetry, which dealt with heroes and grand events, lyric poetry was personal. Lyric poets sang about love, friendship, old age, death, and morality. Some lyric poems were light and humorous, while others were sad, thoughtful, or angry.

The earliest lyric poetry is attributed to a Spartan named Alcman. Alcman is the most famous lyric poet the city-state of Sparta produced. He wrote much of his poetry around 620 B.C. Most of his works that have survived are on only two papyrus documents, and little is known of his other work. He wrote poems

The Douris Painter drew this beautiful scene on a drinking cup. It shows a Greek school scene. On the left a student is learning how to play the lyre. The other student is taking instruction in speech. The drinking cup was probably made in about 480 B.C.

that were meant to be sung by groups of women during rituals and festivals. When Alcman died, he was buried in Sparta, and his tomb survived for several centuries before it was finally destroyed.

Perhaps the first lyric poet was Archilochus of Paros, who lived between 675 B.C. and 635 B.C. He was a warrior-poet. He described his experiences as a soldier, such as the sorrows of losing friends in battle, the fun of drinking and carousing, and the hatred of his enemies. Hipponax of Ephesus, who lived during the sixth century B.C., wrote lively poetry about street brawls, drunken fighting, and poverty. He used colorful slang and street language, which gives modern historians an idea of how ordinary Greek people may have spoken and lived. Alcaeus of Mytilene, who lived from about 620 B.C. to 580 B.C. wrote love songs, hymns, and political poetry that was highly regarded by the Greeks. His poems described everyday life in the city of Mytilene. Much of his work survives today in fragments.

One of the most famous Greek lyric poets was also the only woman known to have written poetry, Sappho of Lesbos. She lived from about 610 B.C. to 580 B.C., and her poetry was deeply respected even during her lifetime. Very little of her work has survived. Historians know of her through other writers, who described Sappho's good reputation and beautiful poetry. Sappho wrote about herself, her friends and family, and how they felt about each other. She also wrote about intimate love between women, the subject for which she is most famous.

## Greek Drama and Playwrights

Of all the types of literature to come from ancient Greece, historians regard drama as the most important. Although there were certainly some kinds of dramatic performances before the ancient Greeks, it was the Greek playwrights and actors who perfected the idea of writing plays and performing them for an audience.

Scholars are unclear as to how Greek theater began. It is likely that the first performances were given by choral groups who sang at religious events. Some performances acted out a scene, such as a fertility ritual. Others praised the god or goddess for whom the ritual was being performed. A playwright named Thespis of Attica is thought to be the first Greek to add an actor to the chorus, which was a major breakthrough in the concept of choral performances. The presence of this actor, called the hypocrite or responder, allowed dialogue to be added to the performance.

The first plays were tragedies. Each year the ancient Greeks held a large festival to honor the god Dionysus that included a contest to choose the best play. Playwrights from all over the Greek world traveled to the festival to compete. Hundreds, perhaps thousands, of tragedies were performed over the years. However, the complete tragedies of only three Greek playwrights exist today.

Aeschylus, who lived from 525 B.C. to 456 B.C., wrote more than eighty plays, but only seven have survived. Thirteen of them won first prize at the festivals. (Later Greek writers recorded the names of the lost plays, which is how modern historians know they existed.) One of his most well-known plays is *Agamemnon*, which is about a hero of the Trojan War. Aeschylus was the first playwright to add a second actor to the stage, thus expanding the possibilities of dialogue.

Sophocles lived from 495 B.C. to 406 B.C. Historians believe he probably wrote about 130 plays, although only seven exist today. Sophocles added a third actor to his plays, allowing for more complex stories and greater drama. One of his plays, *Oedipus Rex*,

**The Theater of Herodes Atticus is located on the Acropolis in Greece. It could hold five thousand people. Ancient writers presented their dramas and comedies in the theater. The theater is still used today.**

# Schliemann and the Treasure of Troy

Heinrich Schliemann may be one of the luckiest archaeologists ever. He discovered the site of Troy, the ancient city described in Homer's epic poems the *Iliad* and the *Odyssey*.

Schliemann was born in 1822. As an adult, he dedicated his life to finding Troy. At the time, most scholars thought Troy was a mythical place invented by Homer as a setting for his colorful stories. Schliemann, however, believed that Troy was real.

Schliemann used a copy of Homer's work as a guide and traveled throughout Greece and the Middle East looking for places that matched the descriptions in the book. He finally found a place that seemed to match Homer's details, an area in the northwest corner of Turkey called Hissarlik. In 1870, he discovered eleven cities buried there, one on top of the other. He declared that one of them was Homer's Troy. Schliemann found gold, jewels, and hundreds of other artifacts. A photo of his wife wearing a group of gold earrings and necklaces from Troy became famous.

Unfortunately, Schliemann was not very careful when he dug, so a great deal of treasure and other artifacts were destroyed. Later, archaeologists argued about which city of the eleven Schliemann discovered was the actual Troy of Homer's poems. Today scientists still debate whether any of the cities are actually the remains of Troy, although some think the one known as VIIA might be the right one. But no one disputes that Schliemann was among the first archaeologists to reveal physical evidence of the Bronze Age civilization.

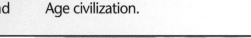

recounts the tragic story of Oedipus, who unknowingly kills his father and marries his mother.

Scholars have only nineteen surviving works of Euripides, who was a contemporary of Sophocles. He lived from about 485–406 B.C. Historians believe that Euripides wrote at least ninety-two plays. His most famous work is *Medea*, a tragic tale of revenge and death. A woman named Medea discovers that her husband Jason plans to abandon her. Medea then kills their children to get revenge for his betrayal.

Even fewer comedies exist today. Scholars know of some ancient Greek comedies, but only eleven complete works have survived. They were all written by the same man, Aristophanes, who lived from about 448–385 B.C. His comedies are filled with humorous references to well-known Athenians of the day that poke fun at Athenian politics and society.

By the Hellenistic period, the Greeks had created an enormous body of literature, including thousands of poems, stories, and plays. Greek writers created works that have influenced and inspired readers from the time they were written to the present day. Unfortunately, almost all of the original copies of these works have disappeared. Many were destroyed by early Christian leaders, who feared the pagan writings of the Greeks and thought them blasphemous against God.

## Chapter VII

# ARTISTS AND ARCHITECTS

The people of ancient Greece filled their cities with beautiful artwork and striking buildings. They carved sculptures that glorified the human form. Expert artists carefully decorated thousands of clay vases with images from myths and legends. Architects and designers imagined and then created some of the most breathtaking structures the world has ever seen. To the Greeks, however, art was part of daily life. There were no great art museums in Greece. In Athens, artists were hired by the government to create religious works for the city. Under these conditions, Greek art flourished and grew.

## Greek Sculptors

Most scholars agree that the Greek style of creating life-size sculpture began some time in the seventh century B.C. Artists created statues of young men at the peak of physical perfection, their muscles rippling with youth, health, and power. Their goal was to create the ideal human form, perfect and beautiful. **_Kouroi_** statues were freestanding figures of naked men striding forward. These sculptures were made of stone. Kouroi are one of the most distinctive art styles of the Archaic

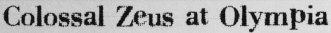

# Colossal Zeus at Olympia

Ancient writers considered Phidias's Zeus, completed for the temple of Zeus at Olympia in about 430 B.C., to be his masterpiece. One Greek, Pausanias, wrote in the second century A.D., "On his [Zeus's] head is a sculpted wreath of olive sprays. In his right hand he holds a figure of Victory made from ivory and gold. . . . His sandals are made of gold, as is his robe. His garments are carved with animals and with lilies. The throne is decorated with gold, precious stones, ebony, and ivory."

Zeus was about seven times life size, standing about 42 feet (13 m) tall. When the statue was finished, it was so enormous that it barely fit into the temple it was made for. Another Greek writer, Strabo, described it in A.D. 18 or 19, saying, "[Phidias] has shown Zeus seated, but with the head almost touching the ceiling, so that we have the impression that if Zeus moved to stand up he would unroof the temple." Some scholars believe that Phidias made the statue gigantic on purpose to create a sense of grandeur and wonder in worshippers.

The statue survived for several hundred years. In A.D. 391, the Christian emperor Theodosius banned the Olympic Games and closed the temples, including the temple of Zeus. The statue was eventually moved to Constantinople, where it was destroyed by fire in A.D. 462. This colossal statue is considered to be one of the seven wonders of the ancient world.

period of Greek history. About two hundred kouroi exist today.

Greek sculptors also created female statues known as **korai**. One of the finest examples of korai sculpture is a statue known as the *Peplos Kore* from the Acropolis in Athens. Historians and archaeologists believe that these statues may have been used as offerings to the gods.

The statue of Zeus at Olympia is considered to be one of the wonders of the ancient world. In the 1700s a German artist, Fischer von Erlach drew this picture of the statue, based on a description from the second century A.D. Greek writer Pausanias. Historians doubt that von Erlach's picture is what the statue really looked like, however.

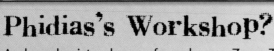

## Phidias's Workshop?

Archaeologists have found a workroom at Olympia that they believe was the workshop of Phidias. In the 1950s, workers discovered a number of terra-cotta molds at the site. They turned out to be molds of the drapery for the robes of Phidias's great statue of Zeus. The molds showed that the gold had been hammered into shape and then decorated with glass. Archaeologists also found a cup inscribed with Phidias's name, further suggesting that the ruins were once the workshop of this great artisan.

Sculptors also created statues of the gods for the temples and oracles. Famous athletes could have their likenesses sculpted for display at Olympia. Many buildings were decorated with a series of carved panels called **friezes** that told stories from mythology and of great events of the day, such as famous battles. These sculptures were brightly painted.

Greek sculptors created their artworks in a variety of materials, including marble, limestone, bronze, terra-cotta, wood, gold, and ivory. Sometimes they combined different materials to make a statue look more realistic. For example, the faces, arms, and hands might be carved from ivory to look like skin, while the clothing might be made from different materials.

One important Greek sculptor was an Athenian named Phidias. Even during his own lifetime, from about 490 B.C. to 430 B.C., he was revered as a great sculptor. Phidias created two great masterpieces of Greek art: a magnificent statue of Athena for the Parthenon and a gigantic statue of Zeus for the temple of Zeus at

Olympia. He has also been credited with designing and sculpting the friezes in the Parthenon, but historians suspect that students and assistants actually created those sculptures. Sadly, neither the Zeus nor Athena statue survives today. However, ancient writers left detailed descriptions of them, and other artists copied them so modern scholars know a great deal about them. The Parthenon friezes still exist and are housed in the British Museum.

## Greek Vase Paintings

Although artists were painting designs on pottery long before the ancient Greeks took up the practice, the early Greeks created their own unique style of artwork for their vases. Some of the earliest Archaic Greek vases were decorated with simple designs such as triangles, checks, and circles. Archaeologists have dubbed this the geometric style, which describes the strict, orderly patterns.

This sculpture of a man carrying a calf is thought to have been from the Greek sculptor Phidias. Most historians believe that no original examples of Phidias's work exist, although there are probably many Roman copies of his work. His statue of Athena, now destroyed, is considered to have been one of his greatest masterpieces.

The Greeks used jars such as this one to serve wine. Jars were decorated with geometric designs and colorful paintings. This jar was probably made in the late eighth century B.C.

In about the seventh century B.C., the patterns changed drastically. Artists decorated the vases with paintings that illustrated stories from mythology and daily life. People were depicted running, riding horses, drinking, playing musical instruments, dancing, fighting, and working.

Fortunately, some artists signed their works, so scholars know the names of a few vase painters. Sophilos was the first vase

The Diosphos Painter painted this beautiful scene on an amphora, which is a large jar. The picture shows several figures from Greek mythology riding a cart pulled by two wild boars. The Diosphos Painter worked during the sixth and fifth centuries B.C.

## Theater at Epidaurus

One of the finest ancient Greek theaters still in existence is the theater at Epidaurus. When it was built, it was famous for its beauty. It is said that the acoustics are so good that someone in the uppermost seats can hear a piece of paper being torn on stage far below. After the demise of the Greek civilization, the theater was forgotten. Slowly, it was partly buried under many layers of dirt.

Archaeologists unearthed it in 1881. Over the years, more excavations have revealed the entire theater, which has been very well preserved. Some parts of it have been reconstructed and restored. The theater is still used today. Each summer, thousands of tourists visit the theater to watch Greek tragedies and comedies performed.

painter whose name is known to modern historians. About sixty intact pots and fragments of his work survive today. Kleitias painted many smaller vases and drinking cups. Historians know that he worked with a potter named Ergotimos because they signed their works together.

In other cases, the potter signed the work, but the painter did not. Therefore, historians have given the painters names, such as the Berlin Painter, after Berlin, Germany, where one of his most famous works is on display, and the Kleophrades Painter, after the name of the potter who made the vases.

Thousands of ancient Greek vases exist today in museums around the world. They are among the only records of daily life from that time period, and archaeologists use them to determine how ordinary Greeks probably lived.

## Architects Transform Greece

Today, many people associate the ancient Greeks with their beautiful buildings. The simple designs and soaring columns of their ancient temples have inspired world architecture since they were first constructed. Even today, a style of architecture called the classical style is modeled after the clean, straight, simple lines and tall columns of Greek architecture. The Parthenon is built in the classical style.

Greek architects overcame many construction problems to create their temples. One problem was size. Greek architects were the first to design columns that could carry the weight of the huge, heavy, stone roofs, for example. Temple designs were simple and based on rectangles, which were very stable. Using rectangles made it easier to build large, safe structures.

Even the ancient Greeks marveled at the skill and talent of their architects. The writer Plutarch recorded the names of some of the architects and artisans who designed glorious buildings, saying "For Callicrates and Ictinus built the Parthenon; the chapel at Eleusis, where the mysteries were celebrated, was begun by Coroebus. . . . Xenocles of Cholargus roofed or arched the lantern on top of the temple of Castor and Pollux; and the long wall . . . was undertaken by Callicrates."

Another great architect was Polyclitus the Younger, renowned in his day for building the magnificent theater at Epidaurus. It is the largest and most magnificent theater built by the Greeks, and it is beautifully preserved today. Polyclitus built it in the fourth

While many ancient structures still stand, little is known about the people who built them.

century B.C., and it was famous in its own time for its beauty and acoustics, or sound quality. The theater could seat fourteen thousand people.

Although modern scholars know the names of a few Greek architects, little information about their lives has survived. Today's historians have only the ruins of the structures they built and brief mentions of their names in ancient writers' works.

# WARRIORS

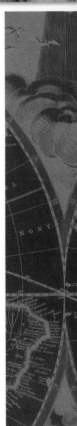

From the earliest days of the civilization, the Greeks battled for control of other lands and to defend their own. From the great Trojan War of Greece's early years to the Peloponnesian War, warfare was a part of everyday life for all Greeks.

## Soldiers of Greece and the Art of War

A great deal of information about early Greek warfare comes from the writings of Homer. His epic poem the *Iliad* tells the story of part of the war between the peoples of Greece and of Troy. The poem is filled with descriptions of mythological events, angry and jealous gods, and a variety of larger-than-life mortal heroes. But the text also includes a great many details of warfare that were probably accurate descriptions of what war was like in Homer's day. Scholars are not sure whether the descriptions accurately describe Greek warfare during later periods, however.

Homeric warfare, according to the poems, was very ritualistic and formal. Rarely did big armies clash with one another, although that is occasionally described. Rather, individual heroes fought one-on-one to determine the course of the war. These heroes only fought others who were as strong and courageous as they were. The warriors usually arrived on the battlefield in chariots, which remained parked nearby. All warriors fought on foot. First, the warriors challenged one

another, sometimes with insults. Then they fought until one was beaten. Sometimes, the loser was killed by his opponent. Other times, he offered the winner a ransom in exchange for his life. The winner had the option of accepting or declining the offer of ransom. If he refused, he could kill the warrior and strip him of his valuable armor. If the winner especially hated the loser, he might defile the corpse by dragging it behind his chariot for all to see.

The various city-states of Greece were continually at war with one another. The two most powerful city-states, Athens and Sparta, were bitter enemies. One of the most famous Greek wars, the Peloponnesian War, was fought between Athens and Sparta, along with many other smaller city-states that allied themselves with one side or the other. The war was fought off and on for about twenty-eight years, between about 431–404 B.C. Finally, Athens surrendered.

Early Greek warriors fought for the glory that victory could bring them. They were less concerned about the wealth and power that came with winning. Greek heroes wanted their

The last great battle between the Spartans and the Athenians during the Peloponnesian War was the naval Battle of Aegospotami, in 405 B.C. The Spartans handed the Athenians a crushing defeat. The Athenians escaped with only twenty out of 180 ships. The Spartans captured and killed thousands of Athenians.

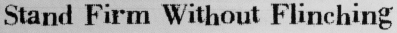

## Stand Firm Without Flinching

Tyrtaeus of Sparta was a patriotic poet. He wrote many lyric poems that roused troops to battle. Tyrtaeus also used them to inspire the Spartans with pride in their city-state and their people. In one poem, Tyrtaeus urges soldiers not to break ranks during battle, saying:

"This is the common good, for the polis [city-state]
and the whole demos [people],
when a man stands firm in the front ranks
without flinching and puts disgraceful flight completely
from his mind
making his soul and spirit endure
and with his words encourages the man stationed
next to him."

bravery and prowess on the field to be celebrated for all time in poetry and story.

### The Military Life of Sparta

The military and the city-state were the center of every Spartan citizen's life from the moment he or she came into the world. The city-state determined whether babies, both male and female, were strong enough to be Spartan citizens. Infants deemed too weak were abandoned in the countryside to die. Although leaving weak or sickly children to die was common in the Greek world, Sparta made it a part of official government policy.

Every male Spartan was taken from his mother at age seven and sent to live in special military barracks. There, boys were taught discipline, athletics, survival skills, hunting, weapons training, and how to endure pain. They lived in these barracks until they were thirty years old. However, after thirteen years of training, at the age of twenty, the male Spartans became soldiers for the state.

The life of a Spartan soldier was one of simplicity, discipline, and sacrifice. A Spartan soldier lived his entire life with his fellow soldiers. He ate, slept, and trained with them. Spartan soldiers were allowed to marry, but they could not live with their wives. When a soldier reached his thirtieth birthday, he became a **homoioi**, or equal. Equals were granted expanded rights and allowed to participate in politics. Any soldier who disgraced himself in any way risked not becoming an equal. Equals were allowed to live in their own houses with their wives and children. However, equals were still soldiers. Military service was required until age sixty.

## New Weapons, Stronger Armies

Beginning in about 700 B.C., the Greeks developed a new style of warfare based on new developments in their armor and weapons. Soldiers during this time were known as **hoplites**, from the Greek word *hopla*, meaning "heavy equipment." Modern scholars know little about how men became hoplites in most Greek city-states.

One of a hoplite's most important pieces of equipment was a large shield called a **hoplon**. A hoplon was made of wood covered by stiff leather or bronze. It was about 3 feet (1 meter) in diameter, which covered half the soldier's body. It was an excellent defense against an opponent's weapons. It not only protected the person carrying it but also partially shielded the solider standing to his left. A line of soldiers carrying hoplons created an

Greek pottery fre-
quently showed soldiers
along with their armor and
weapons. This running hoplite is carrying a shield, a spear, and a helmet. He was
probably painted between 520–510 B.C.

## Athenian Soldier's Loyalty Oath

Most scholars believe that Athenian soldiers were required to take an oath of loyalty when they completed their training. The oath was discovered as an inscription, and it reads:

I shall not disgrace my sacred weapons nor shall I desert my comrade at my side whenever I stand in the rank. I shall fight in defense of both sacred and secular things and I shall not hand down a fatherland that is reduced in size but one that is larger and stronger. . . . I shall be obedient to the laws that are established and to any that in the future may be estab lished. . . . I shall honor the sacred rites that are ancestral.

impressive, glittering wall that was very difficult to break through. Greek foot soldiers were grouped into large, tightly packed formations called *phalanxes*.

The Greeks carried long, iron-tipped spears that were deadly in battle. If a spear tip broke, the soldier simply turned it around and used the iron spike on the other end. Hoplites also carried short swords and wore bronze helmets and leather or bronze body armor.

The new armor and weapons gave rise to a new way of fighting. Most battles during this time occurred on level ground, which made the phalanx formation especially effective. The goal of the hoplite army was to break through the enemy ranks and make them run away. Battle was very simple. Two armies ran across the battlefield and crashed into each other. The larger, stronger side usually won.

Hoplite warfare may have been simple, but it was also ferocious.

**An illustration depicts a phalanx, which is an ancient battle formation.**

When two Greek armies met on the battlefield, a trumpet sounded to begin the battle. The phalanx charged forward, staying in tight formation. When the two sides got close, the soldiers raised their spears. The soldiers in the back began to push against the soldiers in front of them, shoving the phalanx into the enemy. Soldiers on the front lines had little hope of surviving the battle. But every solider had to show remarkable courage, because breaking ranks meant breaking up the phalanx. When the phalanx was broken, the battle was lost.

professions. Using these clues, scholars have pieced together information about Greek slaves and the lower classes.

### An Ordinary Part of Greek Life

In ancient Greece, slavery was commonplace. It was such an ordinary part of life that no one questioned its morality. It is difficult for scholars to know exactly how many slaves were in Athens at any given time, because they did not appear to be any different from the lower-class Greeks who worked alongside them. Most Athenians owned a few slaves. Only the poorest Greeks owned no slaves at all.

A person could become a slave in a number of ways. Most slaves in Athens were prisoners of war. As Greece conquered other lands, the citizens were captured and sold into slavery. In most cases, women and children were sold to wealthy Greeks who put them to work as household servants. Men were sometimes used as household slaves, too, but were usually sent to work in mines or on docks. Often, people were kidnapped and sold into slavery. In Homer's *Odyssey*, for example, a character named Eumaios is kidnapped and sold into slavery as a child.

On occasion, people who owed a lot of money sold themselves or members of their families into slavery to pay off their

## Aristotle on Slavery

The great philosopher Aristotle mentioned slaves in his writings. In approximately 330 B.C., he wrote, "Property is part of the household, and the art of acquiring property is a part of the art of managing the household. . . . And so, in the arrangement of the family, a slave is a living possession."

Many Greek sculptures depict women. This statue shows a woman taking a jewel from a box held by a female slave. The sculpture was most likely made in the late fifth century B.C.

# Workers in Athens

In the "Life of Pericles" from his *Lives*, Plutarch described a variety of Athenian craftspeople and their professions. This description gives historians a good idea of the kinds of craftspeople it took to construct some of the great Athenian buildings.

"The materials were stone, brass, ivory, gold, ebony, cypress-wood; and the arts or trades that wrought and fashioned them were smiths and carpenters, moulders, founders and braziers, stone-cutters, dyers, goldsmiths, ivory-workers, painters, embroiderers, turners; those again that conveyed them to the town for use, merchants and mariners and ship-masters by sea, and by land, cartwrights, cattle-breeders, wagoners, rope-makers, flax-workers, shoemakers and leather-dressers, road-makers, miners. And every trade in the same nature, as a captain in an army has his particular company of soldiers under him, had its own hired company of journeymen and labourers belonging to it banded together as in array, to be as it were the instrument and body for the performance of the service. Thus, to say all in a word, the occasions and services of these public works distributed plenty through every age and condition."

debts. Sometimes babies were left outside to die if their parents could not take care of them. These infants were often picked up and raised as slaves.

Slaves were often treated very well by their masters, depending on what their jobs were. Household servants could become like members of the family and were treated with kindness and love. These slaves were allowed to join the family for private gatherings, rituals, and sacrifices to the gods. Many slaves were given salaries for their work, especially slaves who worked in their masters' factories or shops. Slaves were allowed to save their money to buy their freedom, which many did.

Athens had a class of public slaves who were owned by the city-state. These slaves worked in many government jobs, serving as accountants, clerks, and construction workers. There were also sacred slaves who worked in temples, helping priests and taking care of other duties. For example, sacred slaves assisted in the rituals at the oracle at Delphi.

## Farmers, Laborers, and the Lower Classes

Land ownership was very important to the Greeks. As a result, one of the most respected occupations was farming. By the fifth century B.C., more than half the population of Athens was comprised of small farmers. Most of these farmers worked the land themselves, along with a few slaves. Some large landholders rented their property to poorer farmers, who paid rent in exchange for the right to work the land. Athenians relied on these farmers for food and other products to sustain the city-state. The main crops grown were wheat, barley, olives, and grapes. Athenians also grew produce, such as cabbage, onions, peas, garlic, and figs. Some farmers raised goats and sheep for food and for sacrifice.

In Athens, slaves and lower-class Greek citizens worked in small workshops with another group of people called metics. Metics were free, foreign-born people allowed to live and work in Athens. They could own businesses but not farms because metics could not own land. Many metics were successful business owners. Early writings mention a metic named Kephalos who owned a prosperous shield factory and employed about 120 slaves, the largest factory in Athens. Demosthenes, a well-known Greek orator, was the son of a metic who owned a thriving knife-making factory.

Many Greek vases show people employed in specific professions. Several vases depict forges where workers made weapons, armor, and other metal objects. Some show artists' workshops, in which workers are shown building and polishing statues. Cobblers hard at work making shoes are shown on some vases. Carpenters making furniture and other wooden items are painted on vases as well.

There was no shame in being poor. Even poor Athenian citizens and the citizens of other democratic city-states had the right to vote. All were free to better themselves in any way they could, and many did. This freedom was one of the hallmarks of Greek society and gave it the strength that sustained it for almost a thousand years.

**Greek pottery includes many paintings of women working. These women are gathering fruit. Three of the women hold woven baskets. The painting appears on a cup that was made in the fifth century B.C.**

## Chapter X

# LEGACY OF ANCIENT GREECE

For almost a thousand years, ancient Greece was a powerful civilization formed of many city-states. Greek scholars made advances in philosophy and science. Writers developed new ways of expressing themselves through poetry, theater, and song. Architects designed beautiful structures, such as the Parthenon, that were famous throughout the world. The Greeks believed that they were living in a culture that would last for all time.

But for all of its power and influence, the Greek civilization did not last forever. In the fourth century B.C., a ruthless military commander, Philip, from the Greek city-state of Macedon, conquered all of Greece. His son, Alexander the Great, would follow him to become one of the greatest conquerors of Europe. After Alexander's death, Greece became one of many conquered lands under the rule of foreign leaders. In 146 B.C., Greece became a part of the Roman empire.

But the influence of the ancient Greeks never really ended. Athens remained a center of learning and art long after its military power declined. Greek art became hugely popular with the Romans, who made copies of thousands of Greek sculptures and other artwork. The Romans used mathematics and sciences developed by the Greeks to build their own grand structures. Roman scholars traveled to Greece to study medicine and science.

The rise of Christianity in the fourth century A.D. played a large role in burying much of the Greek culture. Untold thousands of artworks, buildings, and sculptures were destroyed because they were considered to be sinful and pagan. The writings of many Greek scholars were destroyed or forgotten. Advances made in medicine and science were ignored as pagan ideas. It would take Europeans another thousand years to rediscover what they had lost.

In the fifteenth and sixteenth centuries, Italian scholars began to question the authority of the Catholic Church. They wanted to learn about the world without the restrictions Christianity imposed on them, so they began studying the manuscripts of the ancient Greeks. The ideas they contained, such as democracy, philosophy, science, astronomy, mathematics, and medicine, transformed European culture forever. From that point on, Greek culture has continued to influence almost every aspect of cultures throughout the western world.

Today, it is almost impossible to separate the influences of the ancient Greeks from the rest of modern culture. Our ideas of government and politics, our art, our theater and poetry, and the structures we build are all part of the legacy of ancient Greece. The way we think about ourselves and our place in the world come from the philosophies first written by Greek thinkers.

Scientific study and observation that we take for granted today began with the Greeks. Many of the homes we live in and the buildings we work in were modeled after the architecture of the Greeks. Every time we attend a theatrical performance, cheer a favorite runner, gaze at the constellations in the sky, or visit a doctor, we are taking advantage of the legacy of ancient Greece.

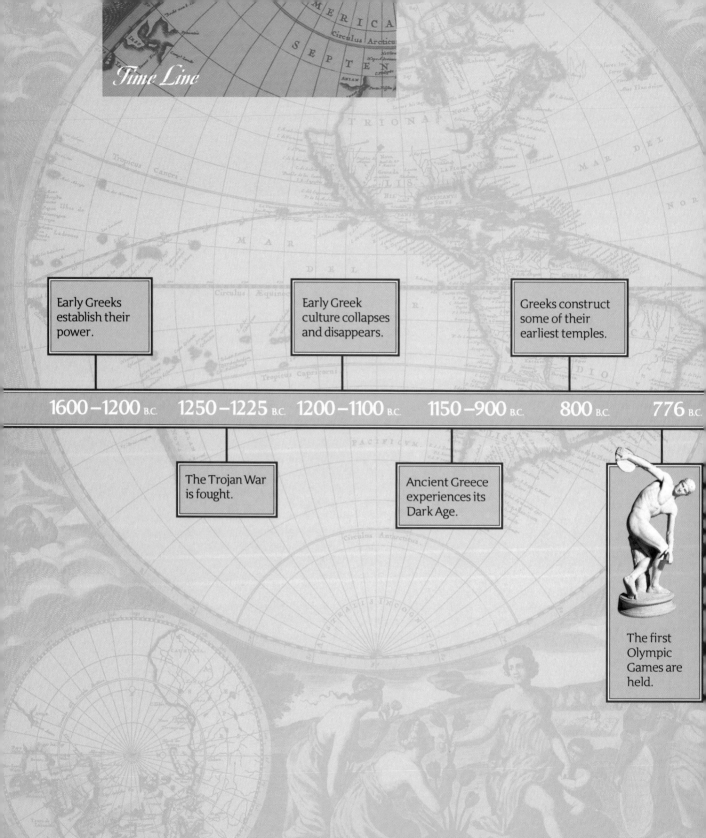

# Time Line

Early Greeks establish their power.

Early Greek culture collapses and disappears.

Greeks construct some of their earliest temples.

| 1600–1200 B.C. | 1250–1225 B.C. | 1200–1100 B.C. | 1150–900 B.C. | 800 B.C. | 776 B.C. |

The Trojan War is fought.

Ancient Greece experiences its Dark Age.

The first Olympic Games are held.

The first Greek city-states are established. Homer composes his epic poems *Iliad* and *Odyssey*.

Solon makes his reforms in Athens.

Cleisthenes establishes democracy in Athens.

**750–700** B.C.　**700–650** B.C.　**594** B.C.　**582–573** B.C.　**508** B.C.　**486** B.C.

Hoplite armies begin to evolve. Early black-figure Greek vases are created.

The Pythian, Isthmian, and Nemean athletic games begin.

Athenians choose archons (administrators) by lot.

Temple of Zeus at Olympia is constructed.

Athens and Sparta fight the Peloponnesian War.

Aristophanes writes the play *Lysistrata*.

**470–456** B.C.  **447–432** B.C.  **431–404** B.C.  **429** B.C.  **411** B.C.  **399** B.C.

The Parthenon is built on the Athenian Acropolis.

Pericles dies.

Socrates is tried and executed.

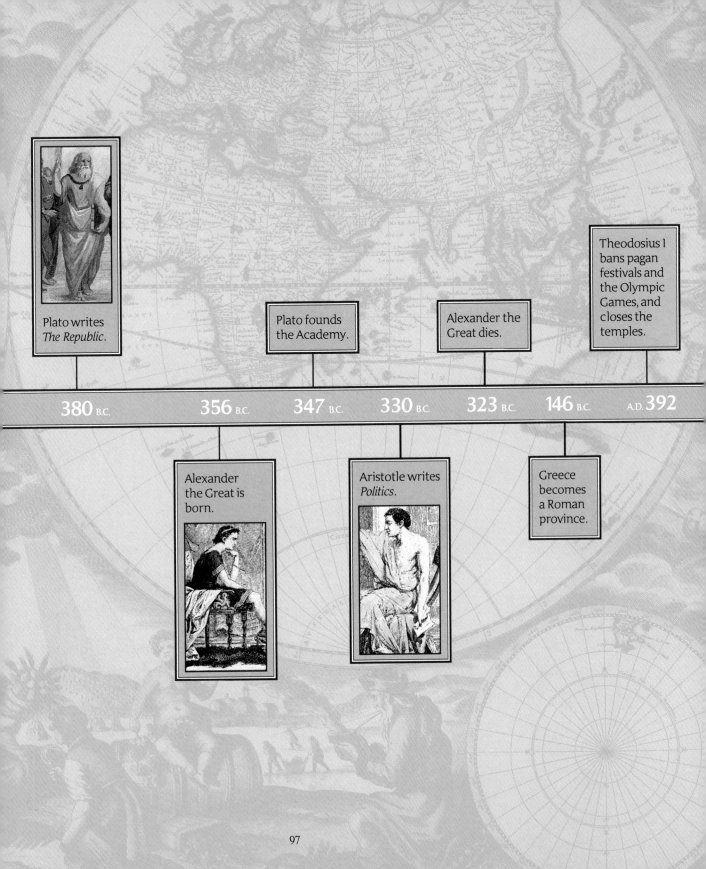

Plato writes *The Republic*.

Plato founds the Academy.

Alexander the Great dies.

Theodosius I bans pagan festivals and the Olympic Games, and closes the temples.

**380** B.C.   **356** B.C.   **347** B.C.   **330** B.C.   **323** B.C.   **146** B.C.   A.D. **392**

Alexander the Great is born.

Aristotle writes *Politics*.

Greece becomes a Roman province.

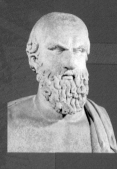

## Aeschylus

### 525–456 B.C.

Aeschylus was Greece's first great tragic poet. He introduced a second actor into Greek drama, allowing for dialogue to be used. Of his approximately ninety works, only seven have survived.

## Archimedes

### 287–212 B.C.

Archimedes is known for his discoveries in mathematics and physics. He developed calculus and studied volume and area. He is famous for using levers on a large scale and for designing a special screw device to lift water.

## Aristotle

### 384–322 B.C.

A student of Plato, he became a teacher at Plato's school known as the Academy. As a philosopher, he believed that every subject could be approached with logic. He developed a type of argument called a syllogism.

## Cleisthenes

### End of the sixth century B.C.

Cleisthenes was a famous Athenian statesman and leader. He established democracy in Athens by giving power to members of the assembly.

## Demosthenes

### C. 384–322 B.C.

Demosthenes is considered to be the greatest Greek orator. Legend says that he spoke with his mouth full of pebbles to improve his diction.

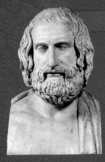

## Euripides

### 485–406 B.C.

Euripides was a Greek playwright whose tragic dramas were famous in his own time. His works focused on ordinary people rather than on heroic figures in Greece's past. Some of his famous works are *Medea* and *The Trojan Women*. He was also interested in philosophy and science.

## Herodotus

### 484–425 B.C.

Herodotus is known as the father of history. He was one of the first writers to record historical events as they actually occurred, not as myths or legends. His greatest work, *The Histories*, was part travelogue, part account of the Persian War.

## Myron of Eleutherae

### Fifth century B.C.

A sculptor, Myron is known for his Discobolus (discus-thrower). The work is famous for its proportion and rhythm. He once created a bronze sculpture of a cow that was so lifelike that people are said to have mistaken it for a real animal.

## Pericles

**495–429 B.C.**

Pericles is considered by historians to be the greatest Athenian political leader. He carried out many governmental reforms, such as paying officials a salary and opening most government offices to all citizens. After negotiating a truce with Sparta, Pericles developed Athens into a powerful, rich city-state.

## Phidias

**c. 490–430 B.C.**

Phidias is considered to be one of the greatest Greek sculptors. He was famous for his statue of Athena in the Parthenon and his statue of Zeus at Olympia. Pericles commissioned Phidias to help direct construction of the Parthenon.

## Plato

**c. 428–348 or 347 B.C.**

A student of Socrates, Plato became a significant philosopher in his own right. He founded the Academy, a university-style school.

## Plutarch

**A.D. 45–125**

Writer and orator, Plutarch once served as the high priest of the Oracle at Delphi. His most famous work, *Parallel Lives*, is one of the best sources of information on ancient Greek leaders.

## Praxiteles

**About 400–330 B.C.**

Praxiteles, a sculptor, created a great variety of works depicting men and gods, male and female. Praxiteles worked in both marble and bronze. Two examples of Praxiteles' work are Aphrodite of Knidos (Cnidos) and Hermes with the Infant Dionysus.

## Socrates

**469–399** B.C.

He was one of the most important philosophers in Greece. He taught his followers to ask questions as a means to learning more about life. The government objected to his actions, and he was convicted of treason and sentenced to death.

## Solon

**Mid-sixth century** B.C.

Solon enacted the first series of reforms that ultimately led to the creation of a democratic government. He abolished the practice of selling oneself into slavery to pay debts. A person's wealth, rather than his social standing, became the deciding factor for participation in political life.

## Sophocles

**495–406** B.C.

His plays established Sophocles as one of the greatest Greek playwrights. Many of his plays, including *Antigone* and *Oedipus the King*, are still performed today. He added a third actor to his plays, creating more opportunity for plot and character development.

## Thucydides

**About 471–400** B.C.

Thucydides, a younger contemporary of Herodotus, was also a historian. His work, *History of the Peloponnesian War*, recounted the events of that conflict. Scholars consider the work to be a fairly accurate account of the war.

**apella** an assembly of Spartan citizens

**asclepions** temples dedicated to the healer Asclepius

*basileus* an early Greek king, tribal leader, or chieftain

*boule* a council of five hundred men

**democracy** a system of government in which every person has a voice

**ecclesia** an assembly of wealthy landowners and warriors in early Greece

*ekecheiria* a three-month truce, agreed upon by all Greeks, so that people could safely travel to the Olympic games

**ephor** a council of five magistrates who watched the king to ensure he did not abuse his power in Sparta. The ephors also had administrative powers in the Spartan government.

**epic poem** a long poem that deals with legendary, historical, or mythical events

**eponymous archon** a civil judge in the early Greek government

**fresco** a large wall painting created by painting onto wet plaster

**frieze** a long, horizontal decorative sculpture or painting

**gerousia** a council of elders in ancient Sparta

*homoioi* a man considered an "equal" with full rights of citizenship in Sparta. *Homoiois* were allowed to participate in government.

**hoplite** Greek soldiers

*hoplon* a large shield made of wood and covered with leather or bronze

**king archon** a member of early Greek government who managed the religious affairs of the state

*korai* life-size female statues

*kouroi* life-size male statues

**metic** free, foreign-born people who lived and worked in Athens

**oligarchy** a system of government in which the state is controlled by a small group of people, usually from the wealthy class

**ostra** pottery shards used by members of the assembly to remove, or ostracize, members of the government. Names of the person to be ostracized were scratched onto the ostra.

**ostracize** to remove from a community or group

**pagan** a person who does not recognize the Christian god

**paidotribes** professional sports trainers in ancient Greece

**palaestra** a school devoted to the training of wrestlers and other athletes

**pankration** a Greek sport that was a combination of boxing and wrestling

**polemarch** the commander in chief of the military forces in early Greece

**polis** the Greek word for "city," also used to describe the independent city-states of ancient Greece

**pythia** the priestess of the Oracle at Delphi

**sophist** a greek traveling teacher

**stoa** a roofed walkway

**tyranny** a form of government in which the ruler is an absolute dictator

## Books

Connolly, Peter. *The Ancient Greece of Odysseus*. London: Oxford University Press Children's Books, 1999.

D'Aulaire, Edgar and Ingri D'Aulaire. *D'Aulaires' Book of Greek Myths*. New York: Doubleday, 1980.

Lasky, Kathryn. *The Librarian Who Measured the Earth*. New York: Little, Brown, & Company, 1994.

Malam, John. *An Ancient Greek Temple*. New York: Peter Bedrick Books, 2001.

Pearson, Anne. *Eyewitness: Ancient Greece*. New York: DK Publishing, 2000.

Solway, Andrew. *Ancient Greece*. London: Oxford University Press Children's Books, 2001.

## Organizations and Online Sites

Acropolis Museum
http://www.culture.gr/2/21/211/21101m/e211am01.html

This museum houses many of the masterpieces of ancient Greek civilization.

Archaeological Museum of Abdera
http://www.culture.gr/2/21/211/21119m/e211sm03.html

This museum contains artifacts from the city of Abdera.

Archaeological Museum at Olympia
http://www.culture.gr/2/21/211/21107m/e211gm04.html

This museum is dedicated to artifacts found in Olympia and in the temple of Zeus.

The British Museum
Great Russell Street
London WC1B 3DG
http://www.british-museum.ac.uk/index_f.html

One of Great Britain's most famous museums, the British Museum houses hundreds of ancient Greek artifacts, including the friezes from the Parthenon, which are known as the Elgin Marbles.

The Metropolitan Museum of Art
1000 Fifth Avenue
New York, NY 10028-0198
http://www.metmuseum.org

Located in New York City, this museum boasts a comprehensive collection of ancient Greek art and artifacts.

The Parthenon
http://academic.reed.edu/humanities/110Tech/Parthenon.html

The Parthenon, one of the most famous structures in the world, is located on the Acropolis in Athens.

## About the Author

Allison Lassieur has written more than forty books about history, world cultures, ancient civilizations, science, and current events. She lives with her husband in Easton, Pennsylvania.